TABLE OF CONTENTS

INTRODUCTION

"Heaven is the place where dreams come true."

—FROM THE FIELD OF DREAMS MOVIE

I have found heaven. Although born and raised in Kansas, I always longed for a horse and the opportunity to live in the West. When I was a young boy, I begged my parents to take a family vacation to the mountains of the West. One summer, my parents drove us to Wyoming and we attended the Cheyenne Frontier Days Rodeo. I was in absolute awe of the cowboys who looked resplendent in their hats, vests, and chaps. We spent time in Wyoming and Montana during that trip, doing some fishing and enjoying the scenery. I went on a horse ride in a tourist place where about ten horses moved down the trail, nose to tail. I vowed one day I would return and make my dream come true.

After many long years of education, I finally moved to Montana with my young family, purchased my first horse, and started to ride. I did not know much of anything about where to ride or how to do it. Many mistakes were made over the years. But fortunately, I am still in one piece and get to ride in some of the most breathtaking scenery in the world. To paraphrase the great cowboy artist Charlie Russell, "If you want to see what man has made, go for a ride in a car. But if you want to see what God has made, go for a ride on a horse."

When I started to ride, there were precious few resources to draw upon. Therefore, I wrote this book so that maybe someone else who has a great love for horses and the beauty of Glacier and Yellowstone National Parks might have a resource to help them.

Most of the trails in Glacier and Yellowstone were created decades ago when horseback riding was much more common. Consequently, most of the trails in both parks are well-suited for horseback riding. Trails that ascend elevation usually have nice switchbacks to make it easier for the horse. In the early days of Glacier and Yellowstone, horseback riding was the preferred method to see the park. In Glacier, thousands of horses were used as tourists rode from one chalet to the next. Tourists would arrive by train to the town of East Glacier (or Midvale, as it used to be known), then ride horses from one chalet to the next as they toured the park. Most of the chalets are now gone. The famous Ptarmigan Tunnel in Glacier was created specifically for the horse rider.

The vastness of Yellowstone with long valleys surrounded by spectacular mountains also was utilized extensively by those on horseback. Tourists would arrive by train to Livingston, Montana. They would then take a rail spur line down to Cinnabar and later, to Gardiner, then ride a horse or stagecoach into the park. Later, another railway reached West Yellowstone, offering a second portal of entry for tourists.

Even today, both Glacier and Yellowstone have guided horse trail rides for those who lack a horse, but wish to see the beauty of either park from the back of a horse.

The information and suggestions in this book are my personal views from years of riding. As the saying goes, "Good judgment comes from experience; experience comes from bad judgment." Unless otherwise noted, for each of the trails discussed in this book, I have been fortunate to ride them with my horse. Therefore, I write from personal experience and thousands of miles on the trail.

I give credit to all those horsemen and horsewomen from whom I have learned so much. In addition, I acknowledge the rangers of Glacier and Yellowstone who have offered advice and been most helpful. They are there to help and I appreciate them for what they do.

Please keep in mind I am describing what works for me, while acknowledging there are other ways to get the job done. There are additional resources available for trail riding, including books, magazines, online resources, and organizations such as Backcountry Horsemen. Both Glacier and Yellowstone have brochures available for the horse rider. These can be obtained at the visitor centers or online. I encourage the reader to study and be prepared, thus making trail riding safer and more enjoyable.

Most of the trails in Glacier and Yellowstone I have ridden multiple times. Each ride is a unique experience because the weather is always different, or the colors, or the wildlife, or my horse, or the company I am with differ. No two rides are ever the same, even if the trail is the same. Each horse ride in a heavenly location such as in Glacier or Yellowstone National Parks is a treasure to cherish and I wish each of you the same gift.

My horse "Scout" in the Belly River Area, Glacier

ACKNOWLEDGMENTS

This book is written with gratitude for my wife LeAnn and my children Audryn, Alyssa, Ethan, and Candyce. They have tolerated and supported my nearly insatiable desire to ride a good horse in beautiful country.

Although there have been many who have helped me in my quest to become a better horseman, none have influenced me more than Buck Brannaman and Ty Heth.

Any profits after production costs will be equally donated between trail maintenance funds for Glacier and Yellowstone National Parks.

Hayden Valley, Mary Mountain Trail, Yellowstone

Horseback Riding in Glacier & Yellowstone National Parks

Revised Edition

Dana P. Damron

Revised Edition

ISBN: 978-1-59152-255-3

Design by Steph Lehmann

Page 11: quote from "The Circle" by Dave Stamey used by permission.

For more information or to order extra copies of this book call (you can add your own information here if you want) Farcountry Press toll free at (800) 821-3874.

sweetgrassbooks
an imprint of Farcountry Press

Produced by Sweetgrass Books
PO Box 5630, Helena, MT 59604; (800) 821-3874;
www.sweetgrassbooks.com

Produced and printed in the United States of America.

29 28 27 26 25 2 3 4 5 6

THESE PAGES: MT. CLEVELAND, BELLY RIVER TRAIL, GLACIER

COVER AND TITLE PAGE: MY HORSE "POCO" AT COSLEY LAKE, GLACIER

THE HORSE

"The air of heaven is that which blows between a horse's ears."

(Arab proverb)

For me, horsemanship is the ability and skill to develop a trusting relationship with the horse, and work together in a manner that is safe and enjoyable for both horse and rider to accomplish the necessary task or job. A rider does not "break" a horse, or even "train" a horse. Horses innately know how to do just about everything we want them to do. The best riders are those who learn how to ask the horse for something and get the horse to respond in a safe and timely manner. It is comparable to a dance in which the rider takes the lead and the horse responds and follows. My horses will do what I ask because they trust I will not ask them to do something they cannot or should not do. When I get on my horse and go for a ride, I am essentially placing my life and health with the horse, so the horse and rider relationship is of the utmost importance.

The horse should be relatively calm and trusting. A horse that is willing and has "try" is priceless. No one breed of horse is best, and mules are also used successfully in the backcountry. An old saying has proven wise: the best color is disposition. When trail riding, a rider will frequently encounter different obstacles that the horse might not be used to. Horses might shy or spook at the shape of a tree stump or a large rock along the trail. Once I was riding with my daughter and we met a couple of hikers who were using a llama as a pack animal. It would be a terrific understatement to say that my horses did not like the llama. Horses will need to cross bridges and water, downed trees, encounter humans and wildlife, unpredictable weather and terrain, and must partner with the rider to have a safe and enjoyable experience.

A horse should have good feet, as trail riding can be hard and increase the risk of lameness. It is preferable to shoe the horse, as rocky trails are common, especially in Glacier. Carrying an "Easy Boot" to act as a spare if a horse loses a shoe is valuable.

Prominent withers are helpful to maintain the saddle in place when riding uneven terrain.

The horse should be used to standing patiently when tied to a hitching post or something else such as a tree. If a horse has a tendency to pull back, it may not be the right horse for trail riding. If a horse is nervous and paws the ground incessantly, it can be destructive to the environment.

Finally, there is no substitute for experience. If the horse is young or inexperienced, it is best to pair up with other horse riders so the horse can learn and gain confidence.

EQUIPMENT

"And the boots I wear are old,
but they have served me well."

—FROM "THE CIRCLE," A DAVE STAMEY SONG

Equipment should look nice, serve the horse and rider well, be functional, and add to the safety and enjoyment of the ride.

1. Horse Gear

Most people ride a Western-style saddle, but Australian-type saddles are also seen in the backcountry. English-type saddles are not preferred for trail riding. The saddle should be comfortable for the rider and horse. When going for a long ride, the stirrups should be set a bit longer than when riding in an arena or working cows. A saddle that is extremely heavy will add weight for the horse to carry over the distance of the trail ride; a lighter saddle might serve you both well.

A saddle pad that can absorb and wick moisture is important, as the horse might perspire a lot if the day is warm or if the horse is not in optimal physical condition and the terrain is rugged. I have found that wool is the best material for saddle pads.

A breast collar is helpful to keep the saddle in place when riding in mountainous territory. If a horse has poorly-developed withers, a crupper behind the horse can help significantly if riding in the mountains, preventing the saddle from slipping forward.

I like to use a snaffle bit with mecate-style reins. This allows for a loop to be used as the reins. If something happens and the rider loses control or drops the reins, they will not fall to the ground as can happen with split reins. If the rider needs to dismount and lead the horse, the mecate has a long tail that can be used to walk or lead the horse. If you ride with split reins, I suggest that you tie them so if dropped or lost, they do not fall to the ground.

As a general rule, I do not like to place a halter underneath the headstall. Most of the time, I prefer to place a halter with lead rope in my saddlebag for use if needed. Alternatively, you can use hobbles for the horse as well, but the horse should be comfortable and used to hobbling before using for the first time out on the trail. Never tie a horse with the reins. I like to use a horn bag to carry items of frequent use or importance. These might include a water bottle, bear spray, snacks or lunch, camera, sunscreen, and bug repellant. I always carry a hoof pick and self-adherent wrap in case my horse needs first-aid due to a scratch or laceration to the leg. Some type of emergency contact device is also very wise. This might be a cell phone, but much of Glacier and Yellowstone National Parks have limited or no cell phone service. Other options include a satellite phone and the "Spot" or "Garmin" messenger systems.

I usually place a cantle bag right behind the cantle of the saddle, especially if I am going on a long ride. I use this to carry rain gear, a halter with lead rope, or perhaps an extra layer of clothing such as a jacket. Saddlebags look nice, but unless properly tied to the saddle, they will bounce and slap the horse when trotting or loping.

2. Rider Gear

A proper-fitting boot that will provide comfort while riding, yet allow for occasional walking, is important. There might be times when it becomes necessary to dismount and walk the horse. I am not a fan of lace-up boots because they will not slip off if the horse rider comes out of the saddle and a foot is trapped in the stirrup. The boot should have a heel that will prevent slippage through the stirrup.

Chaps can be very useful. They protect from the elements such as wind or rain, provide warmth if the weather is cold, and can protect against brush or tree limbs. Chaps also provide friction for the rider against the saddle, such that if the horse spins suddenly the rider is more apt to stay in the saddle.

Always wear a knife and have easy access to it, in case of an emergent need to cut a rope or rein if there is entanglement of horse or rider. A small folding pack saw or axe can come in handy if a downed tree blocks the trail. Always pack rain gear even if the sun is shining brightly overhead and there is not a cloud in the sky.

3. Ride Checklist

- Map
- Knife
- Rain gear
- Sunscreen
- Horse fly spray
- Bug repellant for the rider
- Water
- Snacks
- Hoof pick
- Basic first-aid for rider and horse
- Horse travel papers (Coggins, Brand inspection)
- Camera
- Bear repellant
- Rope to tie horse
- Emergency contact device

Specimen Ridge Trail, Yellowstone

SAFETY

"Better a thousand times careful than once dead."

(Old proverb)

Safety is first and foremost when trail riding. Trail riding is a discipline of horseback riding that requires skill and experience, but anyone can learn if they are willing and apply correct principles during their outing. Experienced horse riders have lost their lives while riding in the backcountry from accidents. It can happen to anyone, but the odds are improved if principles of safety and sound guidelines are followed. The key to safety is awareness.

The old adage from hiking holds true for horseback trail rides: "Plan your ride and ride your plan." That way, others know where you are going if anything unforeseen were to happen.

It is helpful to study maps and trail books. Call or stop by a national park ranger office to inquire about trail conditions. You can also go online and review trail conditions, but they may not always be up-to-date. Carry a map. Most trails in Glacier and Yellowstone have signs at the trailhead with names of trails and distances.

Riding alone can be a sublime experience with your horse. I have found that my horse is usually more attentive and expressive when I ride alone. The horse will depend on you more than if other horses are present. However, if you or the horse are inexperienced, it is wiser and safer to ride with others. An inexperienced horse will feel more comfortable in the presence of other horses. For example, there might be a bridge to cross or a river to ford, and an inexperienced horse may balk. But when the inexperienced horse sees other horses crossing the bridge or the river, it will be a learning moment and the horse will follow and develop confidence.

Always pay careful attention to the horse's emotions. I try to keep one eye on my horse and the other on what lies ahead. If I see something that might pose a challenge, I want to prepare my horse. For example, if I see some hikers coming at us from the other direction and my horse is not aware, I might alert and reassure my horse to the oncoming hikers.

I have only been bucked off once in all of my years and thousands of miles of riding. This happened not from a large moose or ferocious grizzly, but a bird. I was riding a young horse named Scout along the Belly River trail in Glacier when a pine grouse walked underneath Scout from the right side. Just as the grouse reached the left side of the horse, it exploded upward as it took flight. Anyone who has witnessed a grouse take to flight knows this can be an intense moment. As this grouse exploded into flight underneath my horse, Scout became frightened and started to buck. I was caught unaware and quickly came off. Fortunately, Scout did not go far and I was back on the trail. There is no shame whatsoever if it seems prudent to dismount and walk because of a trail obstacle or concern about trail safety. My personal motto is: "If in doubt, dismount and check it out." If I am riding my horse through a large boulder field or avalanche chute filled with large and jagged rocks, I often dismount and walk. My reasoning is that if for any reason my horse would panic or buck that would be a terribly dangerous place to come off the horse. Sometimes a horse does not want to cross a bridge, no matter how much you try to convince him. I have dismounted and walked my horse across the bridge back and forth a couple of times to get the horse used to the bridge, then I mount up and usually we ride across just fine. When the horse balks or reacts to something along the trail, it is an opportunity to help the horse learn and become a better and safer horse. I take advantage of such opportunities to teach my horse and gain experience.

Be careful of crossing rivers and creeks in the spring and early summer, when spring rains and snow melt can lead to high and fast-moving waters that are treacherous to cross. Once, I was riding a great horse named Snappy Jo, an indomitable Arabian mare. We were riding the Red Eagle Lake trail in Glacier. It was early June and I could hear the roar of Red Eagle Creek as we approached. The water was foaming and moving very fast. I did not plan to cross, as I thought we would simply stop and have a look, then probably turn around. I never actually asked my horse to stop, as I thought there was no way she would cross the roaring creek.

My mistake! Snappy Jo never hesitated and when I failed to ask her to stop, she kept right on going and into the creek we went. The water was several feet deep and moving fast. My boots immediately filled with ice-cold water. We made it to the other side and I dismounted and literally poured water from my boots.

When riding in steep country, pay attention to the weight distribution of you and your gear. If the weight distribution is significantly out of balance, there is an increased risk that the horse might stumble. When riding downhill, shift more weight to the hind feet. Conversely, if riding uphill, shift more weight to the front feet. If you are about to ride a steep portion of the trail, up or down, it can be helpful to dismount and check the cinch strap. If too loose, the saddle might slip too much and create a problem. Of course, it is important to avoid over-tightening the cinch as well. And if about to ride a steep portion of a trail, it might actually be wise to dismount and lead the horse through that portion.

If thunderstorms are forecast, be careful about riding in open or treeless high country. Lightning strikes are the number one cause of accidental death among horses. Once, I rode a horse into the Coal Creek country of Glacier, directly underneath Mt. Saint Nicholas. As I enjoyed lunch while sitting on a downed tree, I could see storm clouds gathering. So I mounted up and began the ride back to the trailhead. Alas, the storm hit with a fury and we were pelted with heavy rain. Thunder and lightning were all around, so I decided to dismount and tie my horse to a lodgepole pine tree and wait out the storm.

Suddenly, a bolt of lightning hit very close and the thunderclap was deafening. My mare was frightened and pulled back so hard she pulled the tree right over and it landed on top of her head, knocking her out cold. I thought she had died. I ran to investigate and noted she was still breathing. So I lifted and pushed and was able to get the tree off of her. Slowly, she came to and soon I had her on her feet. The rain was still pouring, but the storm soon moved on. I walked my horse for a while, then mounted and continued the ride. By the time we returned to the trailhead, the sun was shining brightly over the mountains and my horse was lively and acted as if nothing happened.

It is traditional to wear a cowboy hat while riding in the West. The broad brim provides protection from sun or rain. However, for safety reasons, a riding helmet offers more protection to the rider. Head injuries are the most common cause of serious injury or death to the rider while horseback riding. Wearing a helmet is a good idea for everyone, but especially for inexperienced or young riders.

If you must dismount along a trail where one side has a steep drop-off, always dismount on the upper side for safety. Practice mounting and dismounting on both sides of the horse at home in case this is needed out on the trail.

If riding the high country and you encounter a large snow field, be careful about riding the horse across the snow. If the snow field is deep and soft, the horse's feet might sink through. If the horse cannot reach solid ground, it will start to heave and thrash and this can be dangerous.

Always know and follow all rules and regulations of the National Park Service.

PEARLS OF WISDOM

"Whistle, grin, ride."

—RAY HUNT, RENOWNED HORSEMAN AND CLINICIAN.

If possible, try to get started on the ride in the morning, especially during the summer if the trail is likely to be popular with others. Some trailheads have limited parking and if you go early, it can be easier to park a horse trailer. If you start early, there will be fewer hikers on the trail and you will be more likely to see wildlife. If the day is going to be hot, starting early when it is cooler will result in a more enjoyable outing for both rider and horse. In addition, late-afternoon thundershowers are common in the summer and some can be ferocious. It can be tempting to forego packing raingear in the morning if the sky is cloudless, but that can be a big mistake.

When I arrive at the trailhead for a ride, I always follow the same routine before I saddle up. I unload the horse, brush and groom the horse, then lift each foot to check the shoe and clean the foot. It is important to make sure there is no rock or item lodged within the frog of the foot that might cause the horse discomfort or injury. Finally, I apply fly repellant to the horse. In the spring and summer, flies can be numerous and very annoying to the horse. If a horse is distracted with biting flies, it will be less safe and enjoyable for all.

When I place the saddle on the horse and tighten the cinch, I always wait a couple of minutes and walk the horse a few steps, then recheck the cinch strap before mounting. The cinch strap should be firm and snug, but not too tight. Otherwise, a tight cinch can cause soreness and discomfort for the horse.

The best months to ride in Glacier and Yellowstone are July through October. Before July, National Park Service trail crews may not have cleared the trails. In addition, the trails will often be muddy and the higher elevations may have snowpack that blocks the trail. Fall is a great time to ride, as the trails are usually dry and in good condition. The number of tourists and hikers will be reduced after Labor Day, and flies will be much less annoying. But snow can arrive early, so watch the weather forecast as each year is different.

Wildlife can be unpredictable. If riding in Yellowstone, it is a virtual certainty that you will encounter bison. If they are on the trail, I try to wait and see if they will move on. Alternatively, if there is space, I ride around them. Horses that are used to cattle usually fare better. Bison cows and calves will more readily move away, as they tend to be more shy and wary. However, bulls are another matter. They usually stand their ground and are far less likely to move off. Watch the tail. If the tail rises almost straight up and begins to swirl quickly, that is a sign that the bison is nervous or agitated. If bison are blocking the trail and there is no safe way around, then one should retreat and ride back a short distance or so and wait a bit. The bison will almost always move on. Often, they seem to walk very slow, but do not be fooled. They can run faster than a horse.

Both Glacier and Yellowstone have grizzly bears. I have had many encounters with both black and grizzly bears. They are beautiful animals and I always enjoy watching them. The noted bear expert Stephen Herrero has published a book about grizzly bear attacks in North America and says there is no record of a grizzly attacking a mounted horse rider. He considers horseback riding the safest mode of travel in the backcountry where grizzly bears are found.

However, you must still be careful. If a horseback rider comes into contact with a grizzly, the horse might panic and want to flee. It would not be humorous to get bucked off and left alone with the grizzly while your horse hightails it back to the trailhead without you. If you come into contact with a bear at close range, most of the time the bear will leave. Maintain the horse in direct line-of-sight with the bear. However, if the bear is directly in front of you and does not leave, try to keep the horse calm. Back the horse a few steps. Turn the horse a step to the side so that you and the horse appear bigger to the bear. If the bear is guarding an animal kill, it will defend with vigor. Most of the time, the bear will leave or resume whatever it was doing and you can ride on or turn around, whatever seems safest.

If the horse is acting up as if an animal is close by but you cannot identify anything, clap your hands a few times or whistle loudly to let the animal know you are close. If the horse starts to panic and becomes unsafe, I usually try to change the subject. In other words, I do something different with the horse to re-focus the mind. I might turn a sharp circle or two, or change the gait of the horse. However, if the horse seems very unsafe, then quickly dismount and try to calm the horse from the ground. If you need to dismount and walk for a while, make sure you have pepper spray at hand.

Once, I was riding the Slough Creek Trail in Yellowstone when all of a sudden my horse stopped and flared his nostrils. I could tell the horse was on high alert. I looked carefully but could not see anything of concern, so I nudged my horse forward. A few steps later the trail curved slightly and a bear was just ahead on the trail. In this situation, the bear looked at us for a short time, then turned and ambled away.

On another occasion, I was riding from Elizabeth Lake in the Belly River country in Glacier National Park back to the trailhead. We were in the forest and my mare was moving along nicely when all of a sudden she stopped. She was not panicking or nervous, but she was definitely on alert and would not take another step forward. We must have been at a standstill for a good minute. I tried to nudge my horse forward and she would not budge. All of a sudden, a grizzly bear exploded out from under some heavy cover about ten yards to my left and crossed right in front of us and ran away to the right. I thought my heart was going to explode, but my horse remained cool as a cucumber and we merely continued on our way.

Both of these examples demonstrate that horses are often much more aware of our surroundings, including animals that we humans might not ever see. Or in the case of a bear, the horse can be protective for us when otherwise, we might blunder into a dangerous situation.

It may not always be a bear that you see. Another time, when I was riding the Firebrand Pass Trail in Glacier, we came around the trail and a large bull moose was standing a mere fifteen yards away. I was riding an inexperienced horse that I knew would panic and try to run away. So I stopped my horse and tried to reassure him with a friendly pat on the neck. As he stared at the moose, I could feel the tension rise in my horse and he turned to run. I shortened up one rein of the mecate and caused my horse to turn in a short circle, which he did rapidly for several times. I thought I was going to develop vertigo and became nauseated from the rapid motion. Then my horse suddenly stopped and regained his composure. The moose must have thought this was an amusing sight; he turned and left the vicinity.

A more humorous episode occurred when I was riding the trail to Gunsight Lake in Glacier. A deer started to follow us on the trail, staying right behind us for quite some time. So I urged my horse to a trot and we rode another mile or so and the deer stayed right with us. When we came to a creek crossing, the deer must have had enough and stayed at the creek while we continued onward.

Riding in a group of horses with friends can be most enjoyable, but can also increase the risk of complication. The rider out in front should pay attention and act as a leader for those that follow. The lead horse should be calm and set the tone for the rest of the horses. The leader should not start down the trail until everyone has mounted and is ready. Try to keep at least one horse length between each horse. Crowding can increase the risk of injury or mishap. Sometimes a horse in front of another becomes annoyed if the horse behind is too close and will kick.

When riding in a group, everyone should ride at a level that is comfortable and safe for all riders. If one of the horses is unruly or has poor manners, place it last where it can cause the least amount of disruption. If the group reaches a watering hole, all horses should be allowed to have a drink before the leader resumes the ride down the trail. The same rule applies if passing through a gate or across a bridge.

If you need to put on raingear or a slicker while riding, it is best to stop and dismount, especially if the horse is not used to this. If you attempt to put the slicker on while mounted and the wind causes the raingear to flap or flutter, it can spook the horse. This is something that can be practiced at home to improve safety.

When trail riding, do not cut the switchbacks. This degrades the trail and increases erosion.

When encountering hikers coming toward you from the opposite direction, slow down or stop. Be courteous and allow the hiker to step off the trail and allow you to pass. Always thank them for their courtesy. If you come up behind a hiker, again be courteous and send a signal, such as talking, so as not to surprise them. Again, allow them to find a safe place to step off the trail and allow you to pass. Occasionally, a fast hiker might catch you from behind. Find a location where they can pass around you.

Most trailhead or trail destinations in Glacier have hitching posts and outhouses. In Yellowstone, their use is less common. If you need to tie a horse for a relatively brief period of time, perhaps to enjoy the view or have lunch, select a tree that is six inches in diameter or greater, if possible. The old adage "tie 'em high and tie 'em short" is wise indeed. A rule of thumb is to tie the horse "eye high." And select a tree in an area where there will be minimal resource damage to the ground from the horse's feet. If a horse will be tied for an extended period of time, a highline with tree-protector straps is a better option. Do not tie a horse in a campsite area or close to water. If the horse was tied for a while, break up and scatter any manure piles. This reduces flies and parasites for the environment.

If the rider or horse is inexperienced, it is better to select trails that are somewhat easier to ride and postpone the more challenging trails until experience has been accrued.

If you have a steep elevation gain, consider dismounting and walking. This can be helpful to the horse.

Currently, Yellowstone National Park requires day permits for all horseback riding in the park. These can be obtained by calling the Backcountry Ranger Office, or going online. You should call or apply online at least 24 hours in advance. Glacier National Park does not currently have this policy in place.

Backcountry permits are required for overnight trips in both parks. Glacier does not allow for grazing of horses while Yellowstone does. Both parks require weed seed free horse feed such as cubes or pellets within park boundaries. The purpose of this book is not to provide all the detailed information needed for overnight horse camping. Please contact each park for more information regarding regulations.

The Glacier area is known for high winds, especially on the eastern side. More than once, strong winds have caused freight trains to derail in that general area. If winds are blowing strongly, it is suggested that trails leading to a high mountain pass or exposed ridgeline be avoided.

No fishing license is required to fish within Glacier, but a valid Yellowstone National Park license is required to fish within Yellowstone.

TRAIL RIDING

"The trail is the thing, not the end of the trail."

[Louis L'Amour, author]

The trails listed and discussed in this book are those I have found to be most enjoyable for me. They are not an exhaustive list of every possible trail for horseback riding. Unless otherwise noted, I have personally ridden my horse on each trail. For each of the trails, you can ride the full length, or simply ride part way, enjoying the scenery and time with your horse, and then turn around at any point. Most trails have multiple places to stop and relax or enjoy the views.

If considering other trails to ride that are not included in this book, please consult with the National Park Service. Some trails are forbidden to stock animals. In addition, some trails are closed to stock in the early portion of the riding season because of wet trail conditions or because trail crews have yet to clear the trail of downed trees. I have listed current trails in Glacier and Yellowstone that are closed to stock animals, but these might change over time, so consultation with officials is recommended.

Be sure to purchase a park pass when entering and enjoying our national parks. The fees help support and maintain the national parks. Unless otherwise specified, all distances are reported as one-way. Duration is highly variable, dependent on the trail and riding capability. Generally speaking, a horse walks at about 3-4 miles per hour on flat terrain, but is slower if the terrain has elevation gain. Most horses will trot at about 6-8 miles per hour. If the rider elects to trot or lope the horse, you will obviously cover more ground in a shorter period of time. But safety and conditioning of the horse are additional factors to consider if trotting or loping. In addition, when at a trot or lope, there is less opportunity to enjoy the scenery and the risk of mishap with hikers or wildlife is increased. I usually reserve trotting and loping for those areas of trail where it is relatively level and I have a good line of sight ahead of me.

I have not included maps, as there are excellent maps available for purchase online or at outdoor stores located near Yellowstone and Glacier, or at National Park Service Visitor Centers. GPS devices also have maps that can be downloaded and used.

NATIONAL PARK SERVICE INFORMATION:

Glacier National Park

- Website: www.nps.gov/glac
- General Phone: (406) 888-7800
- Mailing Address:
  P.O. Box 128
  West Glacier, MT 59936

Yellowstone National Park

- Website: www.nps.gov/yell
- General Phone: (307) 344-7381
- Mailing Address:
  P.O. Box 168
  Yellowstone National Park, WY 82190-0168
- Backcountry Office:
  Email: Yell_Backcountry_Office@nps.gov
  Phone: (307) 344-2160

Cracker Lake after snowfall, Glacier

TRAILS IN GLACIER NATIONAL PARK

Glacier National Park was authorized in 1910. The name is taken from the glaciers that carved and created the landscape that we see today. Some of the ancient glaciers were thousands of feet thick. Today, only a few small glaciers remain, and they are diminishing at a rapid pace.

Glacier is located just west of the Blackfeet Indian Reservation, and just south of the Canadian border. More trails are located on the east side of the park than the west. In addition, the trails on the east side have more open views, while trails on the west side of the park tend to have long trails through dense forest. The scenery in Glacier is breathtaking and almost beyond description. In general, more hikers will be seen on trails in Glacier than in Yellowstone.

For Glacier, the following trails are closed to stock:

- Avalanche Lake Trail
- Loop Parking Area to Packer's Roost Trail Junction (Granite Park Trail)
- Spur Trail to Sperry Glacier
- Trail of the Cedars Nature Trail
- Hidden Lake Trail
- Logan Pass to Granite Park Chalet
- Appekunny Falls Trail
- Grinnell Glacier Trail
- Hidden Falls Trail
- Josephine Walkway

- Swiftcurrent Lake Nature Trail
- Baring Falls from Sunrift Gorge
- Sun Point Nature Trail
- Dawson Pass to Cutbank Pass Trail Junction
- Running Eagle Falls Nature Trail
- Hole-in-the-Wall Spur Trail
- Huckleberry Mountain Nature Trail
- Spur Trail to Lake Francis

Distances described from end to end means from one end of the trail to the other (one way).

BELLY RIVER REGION FROM CHIEF MOUNTAIN HIGHWAY TRAILHEAD

LOCATION: From St. Mary or Babb take U.S. Highway 89 North to the Chief Mountain turnoff. This will be to the left (west) if driving north. If traveling from Browning, go north on the Duck Lake Road (State Highway 464). After about 35 miles you will reach U.S. Highway 89. Turn right (north) and drive until you reach the Chief Mountain Highway. This is a winding mountain paved road, but it is considered open range and cattle will often be seen along the road, so drive with caution. Once the national park boundary is reached, it is about four miles to the Chief Mountain parking lot, located just before the U.S. and Canadian Customs at the border. The parking lot will be on the left. At the far end of the parking lot is a hitching post, outhouse, and an area reserved for horse trailer parking.

The Belly River country of Glacier is my favorite area to ride a horse. The longer distances lend well to horseback riding. The trails are relatively easy for the horse and the scenery is a spectacular mix of forest and open country with towering mountains looming all around. The remoteness and longer-distance trails generally mean fewer hikers and greater solitude.

1. Belly River Ranger Station

Distance: 6 miles
Degree of Difficulty: Easy
Elevation Gain: Mostly downhill or level to the ranger station, but a moderate climb the last 2 miles on the return ride to the trailhead.

Discussion: A well-defined trail descends from the parking lot through forest for about 2 miles to the valley floor. From there, the trail passes through large, open savannahs interspersed with forest, and the Belly River coursing through the valley. This is very scenic country. In the fall, it is common to see elk, or hear the bugling of bull elk. Abundant aspen trees create a scene of golden beauty in mid-late September.

At the 6-mile mark, the Belly River Ranger Station comes into view on the left, with a large paddock that usually contains National Park Service stock (horses and mules). Take a left toward the ranger station where there is a hitching post. This is a great location to have lunch while sitting on the porch of the ranger station and viewing Mount Cleveland, a towering mountain of 10,466 feet.

2. Dawn Mist Falls

Distance: 2 miles beyond Belly River Ranger Station (8 miles from trailhead).
Degree of Difficulty: Easy
Elevation Gain: Minimal

Discussion: At the ranger station, the trail divides into two forks. One fork leads straight (south) and curves left at the end of the horse paddock and leads to Dawn Mist Falls and Elizabeth Lake. You must cross the Belly River. Follow the sign for the horse ford at the appropriate junction (horse riders will go left, hikers will go to the right and cross a bridge). In early summer, the river might be flowing high and fast

ABOVE: DALY CREEK TRAIL, YELLOWSTONE

FACING PAGE, TOP: MY HORSE AT PEBBLE CREEK TRAIL, YELLOWSTONE

FACING PAGE, BOTTOM: FRIENDS RIDING ON SPECIMEN RIDGE TRAIL, YELLOWSTONE

PREVIOUS PAGE: HELEN LAKE, GLACIER

Above: **Cosley Lake, Glacier**

Right: **Hellroaring Creek with my horse Belle, Yellowstone**

Facing page, top: **Specimen Ridge Trail with my daughter, Yellowstone**

ABOVE: *Boulder Pass, Glacier*

FACING PAGE, INSET: *Lee Ridge Trail with my son and nephew, Glacier*

FOLLOWING PAGE: *Iceberg Trail, Glacier*

from snow melt. But later in the summer or come fall, the river is more mellow and very easy to ford. At the falls, there is a sign and trail cut-off that veers left. Dismount and tie the horse near the main trail and walk down to the falls. It is a short walk but well worth the visit.

3. Elizabeth Lake

Distance: About 3.5 miles beyond Belly River Ranger Station, or 9.5 miles from the trailhead.
Degree of Difficulty: Easy
Elevation Gain: Minimal

Discussion: Continue on the main trail from Dawn Mist Falls. The foot of Elizabeth Lake is about 9.5 miles from the trailhead, a long day ride. There are hitching posts with horse camping available at both the foot and head of Elizabeth Lake, a beautiful destination with outstanding fishing for rainbow trout and artic grayling. If horse camping at Elizabeth Lake, be sure to take the opportunity to ride to Helen Lake, about 2 miles south of Elizabeth Lake. This is a beautiful lake with Ahearn Peak looming overhead. Moose and bears frequent this area. If I had one horse ride left in my life, I would choose to ride to Elizabeth Lake.

4. Cosley Lake

Distance: About 2 miles from Belly River Ranger Station, or about eight miles from the trailhead.
Degree of Difficulty: Intermediate
Elevation Gain: Minimal

Discussion: At the Belly River Ranger Station the trail divides into two forks. For Cosley Lake, turn right immediately after crossing the bridge just before the ranger station. After riding about 0.25 mile, you must cross the Belly River. A suspension bridge for hikers is to the left (south), but stay right and follow the signs for the horse ford. In spring or early summer, the river may be high from snowmelt or rain, but by mid- to late summer, the river is generally passable with stable footing for the horse. After crossing the river, it is about 2 miles to Cosley Lake. There is some elevation gain, but it is not severe. Gros Ventre Falls is about 0.5 mile before Cosley Lake. This waterfall has a steep drop that exceeds 100 feet, and in spring or early summer it can be heard roaring mightily before it is actually seen. Cosley Lake is a beautiful destination for lunch or horse camping. A hitching post is present at the lake. A rider may also continue onward to Glenns Lake and beyond but the distances involved make it impractical for day rides.

Note: one can also do a long ride with a partial loop by riding to the Belly River Ranger Station. Then cross the Belly River and ride to Cosley Lake to enjoy the views. Then backtrack a short distance, and there is a cut-across trail that leads to the Elizabeth Lake trail. Once this trail is reached, turn right and continue on to Elizabeth Lake. When ready, can turn for home and ride back to the Chief Mountain trailhead. This makes for a long day of riding, but the scenery is spectacular.

5. Lee Ridge and Gable Pass Trail

Distance: 6 miles (to the pass)
Degree of Difficulty: Intermediate
Elevation Gain: 2,200 feet

Discussion: About 0.25 mile east of the Chief Mountain parking lot is the trailhead for the Lee Ridge Trail. You can park in the main Chief Mountain parking lot, or there is a pullout along the road about 0.25 mile up from the parking lot on the north side of the road. The Lee Ridge trailhead is on the south side of the road. The trailhead can be difficult to locate among the trees, but there is an orange marker nailed to a tree, and a National Park Service sign at the trailhead. The trail winds through the forest for several miles before climbing atop the open and broad Lee Ridge. The views are spectacular, as the Belly River country is visible to the west, while Chief Mountain looms just to the east. You can ride around and explore on the broad ridgetop, including a ride to Gable Pass. I suggest riding no more than about 5 miles or so, which will keep you from losing elevation. There are wonderful areas to dismount, relax, enjoy the views, then return. Although the trail eventually continues down to the Belly River Ranger Station, it is not recommended that horses descend that portion of the trail as it is steep and not very suitable for horses. This is not a good trail to ride if the wind is blowing vigorously, as the Lee Ridge is exposed and open.

MANY GLACIER

Location: From St. Mary take U.S. Highway 89 North, or from Browning take Duck Lake Road and travel to Babb. Follow signs to Many Glacier. At Swiftcurrent Dam, take a left toward Many Glacier Lodge, then another left up a drive into a large parking lot for the trailhead to Piegan Pass or Cracker Lake. However, if going to Iceberg Lake, Ptarmigan Tunnel, or Swiftcurrent Pass Trails, proceed straight at the turnoff for the lodge. Continue to the end of the road where another parking lot is located. Do not turn into the small loop for the Iceberg Lake trailhead, but rather, park in the large parking lot at the end of the road.

The Many Glacier area is perhaps the most stunning and beautiful of all the areas in Glacier. It is also among the most popular. If planning a ride during July or August, it is best to arrive early in the morning, as parking for a horse trailer can be a challenge later in the day.

1. Cracker Lake

Distance: 6 miles
Degree of Difficulty: Intermediate
Elevation Gain: 1,120 feet

Discussion: Many people consider Cracker Lake as a favorite horse riding trail, including a horse concessionaire located at the trailhead.

The trail winds through forest and open areas as it circumnavigates the Sherburne Reservoir. Do not take the Cracker Flats loop, but veer right and continue onward toward Cracker Lake. This initial portion of the trail will often be in rough shape from the heavy horse traffic from the horse concessionaire. But after the Cracker Flats loop trail, the quality of the trail generally improves significantly. The trail consistently gains elevation, but has well-built switchbacks. Cracker Lake is excellent bear country. Once, I saw seven grizzly bears on a ride to Cracker Lake in October. There is a hitching post at the lake. Cracker Lake is a brilliant turquoise blue and surrounded by a towering cirque. Bring your camera. . .and bear spray! This trail is extremely popular in the summer, so go early to obtain a parking spot for the horse trailer.

2. Piegan Pass

Distance: 8 miles
Degree of Difficulty: Challenging
Elevation Gain: About 2,500 feet
Discussion: Although Piegan Pass can be accessed from the Going to the Sun Road at Siyeh Bend, horse riders should begin the trail in the Many Glacier Valley.

The trail elevation is significant and this trail requires a well-conditioned horse. However, the trail is otherwise good. Once atop the pass, the views are stunning and the riding is much easier. My preference is to ride to Piegan Pass from Many Glacier, then ride over to Siyeh Pass, then turn around and return to Many Glacier.

3. Ptarmigan Lake and Tunnel

Distance: 5 miles
Degree of Difficulty: Challenging
Elevation Gain: About 2,500 feet

Discussion: The trail to Iceberg Lake and Ptarmigan Lake and Tunnel are the same for the first 2.3 miles until Ptarmigan Falls is reached.

The first 0.5 mile is steep and it might be best to walk the horse. Once the main trail is reached, the trail will be quite level and easy-going for the remainder of the journey to Iceberg Lake, while the trail to Ptarmigan Lake will involve elevation gain. There is a solid bridge across Ptarmigan Creek that allows for the passage of horses. A short distance past the bridge is a fork. Go right for Ptarmigan Lake and the Ptarmigan Tunnel. Go straight to reach Iceberg Lake.

The trail to Ptarmigan Lake and Tunnel climbs through forest for a couple of miles. This is excellent bear country, so be alert. The lake itself is located in a beautiful cirque. To continue to the tunnel, follow the trail around the left side of the lake. There's some elevation gain, but the trail has nice switchbacks and is quite doable for horses. However, a horse that is overweight and out of shape will struggle. At the tunnel, dismount to enjoy the views, then walk or ride the horse through the tunnel to the far side for outstanding views of the Belly River Valley and Mt. Merritt. If you want to do a long loop ride, continue down the trail to Redgap Junction, then turn right and ride to Poia Lake, continuing on to Many Glacier. You can also ride on to Elizabeth Lake, which is visible from the north side of the tunnel.

The Ptarmigan Tunnel was built in the 1930s, specifically with the horse in mind. To ride to the tunnel invokes a sense of history and respect for those who built the tunnel. From the Ptarmigan Lake side of the tunnel, spectacular views of Mt. Wilbur and the Ptarmigan Wall await. On the far side of the tunnel, outstanding views of Mt. Merrit, Elizabeth Lake, and the Belly River country are not to be missed.

4. Iceberg Lake

Distance: 5 miles
Degree of Difficulty: Intermediate
Elevation Gain: About 1,190 feet

Discussion: The ride to Iceberg Lake is one of the most scenic and popular in the park. There is a hitching post at the lake. The ride will be most enjoyable if started early in the morning, before the majority of hikers have started their hike, or if performed in the fall when the number of tourists has decreased. If this ride is performed in July or August during the midday, you can encounter hundreds of hikers. For this reason, it might not be the best trail to ride during the busy season. In addition, parking for a horse trailer in July and August will be very difficult to obtain.

5. Swiftcurrent Pass

Distance: 6.5 miles
Degree of Difficulty: Challenging
Elevation Gain: 2,250 feet

Discussion: The trailhead to Swiftcurrent Pass is located near the trailhead for Iceberg Lake at the far end of the parking lot in the Many Glacier area.

Although it is about 8 miles to the pass, you can ride about 4 miles to the head of a valley and enjoy a very easy-going trail with stunning views, towering mountains, and beautiful lakes. Fishercap, Redrock, and Bullhead Lakes are easy destinations and prime moose habitat. There is a spur trail to Redrock Falls. Other, unnamed waterfalls often gracefully cascade down the steep mountain slopes, especially in late spring and early summer. You can explore the valley, dismount and enjoy time at the lakes, and then return to the trailhead. Or you can proceed to the pass.

At the head of the valley, the trail begins a steep ascent to Swiftcurrent Pass. I suggest intermittent dismounting and walking the horse, as the grade is steep. However, the trail is safe with plenty of switchbacks. Once atop the pass, the views are impressive. You can ride on to the junction with the Highline Trail or the trail to Fifty Mountain. Both of these trails are level and easy-going. Though it is not realistic to ride very far up those trails as part of a day ride originating from Many Glacier, it would be very pleasant with gorgeous views to ride a mile or two toward Fifty Mountain. If riding to Swiftcurrent Pass or beyond, plan to ride in August or September as there can be large amounts of snow in the high country. The last time I rode this trail I made it to the pass just fine, but once we headed up the Fifty Mountain Trail, we had to turn around on account of a massive snowdrift that blocked the trail.

6. Poia Lake

Distance: About 6.5 miles
Degree of Difficulty: Intermediate
Elevation Gain: 1,350 feet

Discussion: The trailhead is located near the Apikuni Falls trailhead on the Many Glacier Road, about 0.5 mile before the turnoff to the Many Glacier Hotel. Parking for a horse trailer is very difficult right at the trailhead. It is best to find a pull-out somewhere along the road.

The trail is not difficult for horses and passes through forested and occasional open areas. This trail is moderately low on scenic value but makes for a pleasant ride on a trail that will be less crowded than other trails in the Many Glacier Valley.

St. Mary Valley

The St. Mary Valley is the east-side access for the Going-To-The-Sun Road. There are hotels, restaurants, and a National Park Service Visitor Center.

1. Red Eagle Lake

Distance: About 7.5 miles
Degree of Difficulty: Easy
Elevation Gain: 300 feet

Discussion: The trailhead for Red Eagle Lake is located just west of St. Mary's Lodge and Resort, just before you reach the Glacier National

Park entrance station. There is a dirt road that heads south (left) and a small parking lot with a sign marks the trailhead.

It is about 8 miles to the lake, but the trail is gentle and easy-going as it passes through forest and open meadows. Views of St. Mary Lake and the area's towering mountains are breath-taking. Areas along the trail and around the lake were hit hard by a large fire in 2006, offering riders a glimpse of fire as part of the cycle of life in the wild. This is one of my favorite rides.

2. Gunsight Lake

Distance: About 6 miles
Degree of Difficulty: Intermediate
Elevation Gain: About 1,500 feet

Discussion: If planning a ride to Gunsight Lake, the best place to park is the Sun Point parking lot where there is plenty of room for trailers. At the far west end of the parking lot, there is a trailhead with signs.

Follow the trail along the north shore of the lake until you reach a junction. Veer left and follow the trail to Gunsight Lake. The trail to Gunsight Lake is mostly in the forest and is of limited scenic value. However, the lake is a tremendous destination. It is one of the most beautiful high-mountain lakes in Glacier. The fishing is outstanding. The trail to Gunsight Lake is mostly in the timber. But there is the beautiful Florence Falls, and an open grassy meadow with beautiful views of Mt. Jackson. Gunslight Lake is a tremendous destination. One can also ride to Gunsight Pass for spectacular views, but this involves another 1,500 feet in elevation gain and another 1.5 miles.

I have ridden a horse to Gunsight Lake several times. A couple of times, I packed a float tube and fly rod, and fished the lake. Fishing is difficult from the shoreline, as there is little room to cast a fly rod. But with a float tube, the opportunity to float and fish, surrounded by towering mountains, must be what heaven is like.

3. Siyeh Pass

You can also ride to Siyeh Pass from the Going-to-the-Sun Road. The trail is filled with gorgeous scenery, but parking for a horse trailer is very difficult. Siyeh Pass is better accessed from the Many Glacier area via Piegan Pass, which is a longer trail but better for horses and parking.

CUT BANK CREEK

Location: The turnoff is located on U.S. Highway 89, midway between Browning and St. Mary. Alternatively, a rider can drive north from Browning on Duck Lake Road and turn west (left) at the Star School Road. Drive to the junction with Highway 89, and directly across the highway is the road into the Cut Bank Creek area. This is a gravel road of about 5 miles to the Glacier boundary line. From there, it is about 1 mile to a National Park Service cabin and campground. There is a common trailhead for hikers and horse riders and ample room for horse trailers.

This is one of my favorite locations to ride, as the Cut Bank Creek area is much less traveled and visited than other trailheads in Glacier, yet the scenery is outstanding. The peaks of Mad Wolf and Bad Marriage Mountains loom overhead.

The common trail leads west from the parking area. It is approximately 4 miles to a trail junction. Most of this trail is through forested areas, but occasional open areas provide visibility to beautiful vistas.

1. Triple Divide Pass

Distance: 7 miles
Degree of Difficulty: Challenging
Elevation Gain: About 2,400 feet.

The first several miles of this trail are mostly in the forest and not very scenic, but great views await. At the trail junction at the 4-mile mark, go right. Atlantic Creek Campground is visible shortly thereafter.

Triple Divide Trail and Pass, Glacier

In about 1 mile, there is a second trail junction. Go right for the trail to Triple Divide Pass. This is a rugged climb that involves significant elevation gain. There are no switchbacks, as the trail is carved alongside the mountain the entire way. Although safe for horses, this trail is not for the faint of heart. However, once you reach the pass, the views are heavenly and well worth the effort. The trail to Triple Divide Pass should not be attempted before mid-July, as residual snowdrifts from the previous winter will likely remain.

Triple Divide derives the name from the three water drainages that exist on nearby Triple Divide Peak. This is referred to as a hydrologic apex. Depending on the location, water from Triple Divide Peak can drain into the Pacific Ocean via Pacific Creek which flows into the Flathead River, the Atlantic Ocean via Atlantic Creek which drains into Cut Bank Creek and ultimately the Missouri River, or the Arctic Ocean via Hudson Bay Creek which flows into the St. Mary River and north into Canada.

2. Medicine Grizzly Lake

Distance: 6 miles
Degree of Difficulty: Easy
Elevation Gain: About 500 feet

At the main trail junction, go right and then onward to Medicine Grizzly Lake. At the second trail junction, about a mile or so up the trail, veer left for the lake (the right branch leads to Triple Divide Pass). Just prior to the lake is a large meadow which affords beautiful views of the surrounding mountains. Medicine Grizzly Lake is known for great fishing.

3. Morningstar Lake

Distance: 5 miles
Degree of Difficulty: Intermediate
Elevation Gain: About 900 feet

At the main trail junction, go left to Morningstar Lake. You will pass Atlantic Falls along the way. Morningstar Lake is small but very pretty. Mountain goats are commonly seen in the cliffs overlooking the lake. If you have the time and energy, you can ride on to Katoya Lake and Pitamaken Lake. However, this portion involves significant elevation gain. The reward is that there will be very few visitors except for wildlife. I have probably ridden this way a half-dozen times and not once have I seen another person. This is excellent bear country.

TWO MEDICINE

Location: This trailhead is located at the Two Medicine area of Glacier. The road is accessed from the small village of East Glacier. Parking for horse trailers is best accomplished in the Scenic Point parking lot as other parking areas are likely to be full or not ideal for horse trailers.

1. Upper Two Medicine Lake

Distance: 5 miles
Degree of Difficulty: Easy
Elevation Gain: 300 feet

Discussion: For the ride to Upper Two Medicine Lake from the foot of Two Medicine Lake, there are two trails. My suggestion is to ride along one side of Two Medicine Lake to Upper Two Medicine Lake, then return via the other side, making a loop. The ride will be mostly in the forest with occasional views that are spectacular. Upper Two Medicine Lake is a very pleasant destination for lunch or to relax.

2. Old Man Lake

Distance: 6.5 miles
Degree of Difficulty: Intermediate
Elevation Gain: About 1,850 feet

Discussion: The trail to Old Man Lake is one of the most beautiful in the park, and the fishing can be excellent to boot. Access the trail by parking in the Scenic Point parking lot. This is preferred for horse trailers. Saddle the horse and ride down the road a short distance and turn right at the Ranger Station. Continue down the road and cross the outlet creek at the foot of Two Medicine Lake, then wind your way through the willows to the main trail. Old Man Lake trail will be to the right; Upper Two Medicine Lake will be to the left. The ride to Old Man Lake will curve around Rising Wolf Mountain before heading up the Dry Creek Valley and towards Old Man Lake. The ride through Dry Creek Valley is fantastic. The last mile or so involves some elevation gain and is mostly in timber. In the late summer or early fall, huckleberries abound. There is a hitching post for horses. Tie the horses, then walk to the lakeshore and enjoy the views with Flinsch Peak looming overhead.

But beware for bears. Once, I rode to Old Man Lake in the fall for some fishing. I was acutely aware of the possibility of bears. I was alone when we arrived at the lake, so I rode my horse to the lake and carefully looked around. I did not see any bears, so I rode back to the hitching post. I assembled my fly rod, donned waders, and walked back to the lake. And right there in front of me was a large grizzly bear. Both of us were surprised to see the other. I yielded the lake to the bear, returned to my horse, and rode back the way we came.

3. Cobalt Lake and Two Medicine Pass

Distance: 5.7 miles to Cobalt Lake, 2 miles to Two Medicine Pass.
Degree of Difficulty: Intermediate to Cobalt Lake, challenging to Two Medicine Pass.
Elevation Gain: About 1,400 feet to Cobalt Lake, another 1,100 feet to the pass.

Discussion: Cobalt Lake is not very large, but sits below towering mountains and makes a great destination ride. It is moderately steep in a couple of places, and the ride to the lake is mostly through forested areas. The trail to Cobalt Lake begins on the south side of Two Medicine Lake, near the boat dock. It is best to park in the Scenic Point parking lot and ride down to the trailhead. At about the 3.5-mile mark, there is a junction with Rockwell Falls Trail. From Cobalt Lake, it is a little over 2 miles to Two Medicine Pass. It is steep, but the trail is safe for horses and the views from the pass are well worth the effort if you have the time. Wildflowers are often abundant during mid-summer. However, the pass should be avoided if high winds are blowing.

Being the hard-core rider that I can be, I once arose well before dawn and was at the Two Medicine Lake trailhead with my horse at first light. My Arabian mare Snappy Jo and I rode to Cobalt Lake, then up and over Two Medicine Pass and down to Lake Isabel. I brought along a fly-fishing rod and caught about a half-dozen cutthroat trout in the space of an hour. On the ride back, there was a large herd of mountain sheep atop Two Medicine Pass. After descending to Cobalt Lake, my mare spontaneously broke into a trot at Cobalt Lake and did not stop until we reached the trailhead. I think she was anxious to get home!

SOUTHERN GLACIER

1. Firebrand Pass and Ole Lake

Distance: 5 miles to Firebrand Pass, about 8 miles to Ole Lake.
Degree of Difficulty: Challenging
Elevation Gain: 1,950 feet

Discussion: The trailhead for Firebrand Pass begins at about mile-marker 203 along U.S. Highway 2, west of East Glacier. There is a parking area between the highway and the railroad tracks. Trains pass frequently and you should be alert so that the horses are prepared if a train suddenly appears. Trains going west at this location are going up to the continental divide and the engines will be loud. Trains headed east are going down from the continental divide and are much quieter. So be careful and be aware. I suggest saddling the horse, then walk the horse across the rail tracks to a gate in the fence where the trail begins. Open the gate and lead the horse through, then close the gate behind you. You are now ready to ride.

Initially, the trail is an old road for about 0.5 mile, and then it merges into a trail. A little over 1 mile down the trail, there is a junction. To the left is the Autumn Creek trail; to the right is the path to Firebrand Pass.

This is another of my favorite areas to ride. Because relatively few visitors frequent the area, there's a greater opportunity for solitude than other areas. It is very pretty here in the fall as there are numerous aspen trees that turn a brilliant golden color.

The trail winds upward through a mixture of forest and open areas. If riding in June or July, there will likely be snowfields to cross—massive drifts that formed during the previous winter and spring. These snowfields should be approached with caution. The horse can slip and slide. In addition, if there is a soft spot, the horse's leg(s) might fall through the snow; the horse can get stuck and panic and thrash.

The actual pass is not visible until you wind around the edge of Calf Robe Mountain. The trail has several switchbacks and is only accessible by a strong horse. At the summit of the pass, the winds can be ferocious, so hold onto your hat. A rider can continue down the other side of the pass to Ole Lake, about 3 additional miles. This lake has easy fishing for small cutthroat trout. I have ridden to Ole Lake a couple of times and taken a small frying pan with a cook stove. I caught a few fish and fried them for a nice lunch, then turned around and rode home.

2. Upper Park Creek and Lake Isabel

Distance: About 15 miles to Upper Park Creek cabin and campsite, about 17 miles to Lake Isabel.

Degree of Difficulty: Easy

Elevation Gain: About 800 feet to Upper Park Creek Campground, about 1,000 feet from the campground to Lake Isabel.

Discussion: Upper Park Creek and Lake Isabel are not a good choice for a day ride because of the trail length. This is a great trip for horse camping in a secluded area of Glacier. I suggest riding to Upper Park Creek campground and setting up a base camp on day one. The next day, ride to Lake Isabel and plan to fish and enjoy the views. The fishing is outstanding. Check with park rangers about trail conditions before departure. It's a good idea to pack a saw as downed trees are sometimes a challenge.

3. Coal Creek

Distance: Up to 8 miles
Degree of Difficulty: Easy, but requires a major river crossing
Elevation Gain: Minimal and gradual

Discussion: The Coal Creek trailhead is located near Stanton, about 16 miles east of West Glacier. There is a hitching post and small parking area on the south side of U.S. Highway 2. Saddle the horse, then walk across U.S. Highway 2 and take the old dirt road trail down toward the river. You must cross the railroad tracks. Then turn back to the right and look for a fence post along the river that marks where the horse ford is located. Cross the Middle Fork of the Flathead River at the fence post. This trail is best accessed in late summer or fall, when the river flows are slower and lower.

The trail winds through burnt forest and you will cross Coal Creek several times. The trail is not particularly high in scenic value, but there are views worth the ride and it will be very solitary. The beautiful Mt. Saint Nicholas looms large, giving you great views. In October, the tamaracks (western larch) turn a resplendent yellow, filling the valleys with a golden hue. I have been on this trail several times and never once seen another hiker or rider. I like to ride about 6 or 7 miles in until I am right below Mt. Saint Nicholas.

You can ride on to the Martha's Basin area, which includes Buffalo Woman and Beaver Woman Lakes but the scenic value is low and the two lakes are fishless. I found this out the hard way when I once rode my horse and packed into this area. I was hoping for a glorious fishing trip. I spent a lot of time fishing but never had a single bite to my fly rod, nor did I see any evidence of a fish. I returned home quite disappointed, then read in a book that neither lake had fish.

WESTERN GLACIER

1. Head of Bowman Lake

Distance: About 7 miles
Degree of Difficulty: Easy
Elevation Gain: Minimal

Bowman Lake is a beautiful and large lake on the west side of Glacier. There is a National Park Service corral available for horses at Bowman Lake, but you must make a reservation ahead of time by contacting the Polebridge Ranger Station. I have reserved the corral, parked my trailer right there, and camped in the nearby auto campground. From the corral, you can ride up and along the north side of the lake. At the head of the lake, there is a backcountry campground with a hitching post. You can do a day ride to the head of Bowman Lake and return to the trailhead, or camp for the night. However, a backcountry reservation is required if camping in the backcountry.

Once, I rode to the head of Bowman Lake with a packhorse and camped for the night. The next morning, I arose early and rode my saddle horse to Brown Pass, then around to Hole-in-the-Wall and the Boulder Pass region. This is some of the most spectacular scenery in all of Glacier.

2. Quartz Lakes

Distance: About a 13-mile loop, round-trip
Degree of Difficulty: Intermediate
Elevation Gain: 1,500 feet

From the Bowman Lake Campground, you can also ride to Quartz Lakes. This can be performed as a loop ride. (Note: I have not actually ridden this trail.)

3. Kintla Lake and Upper Kintla Lake

Distance: About 6 miles to Kintla Lake, about 9 miles to Upper Kintla Lake.
Degree of Difficulty: Easy
Elevation Gain: Minimal

Kintla Lake is a stunningly beautiful lake, located in the northwest region of Glacier. From the trailhead, it is about 6 miles to the head of the lake. But the ride is mostly through forest and not especially scenic. In addition, there is no horse corral and the campground is not suitable for horse trailers. The ride to Upper Kintla Lake is about 2.5 miles past the head of Kintla Lake. This lake is situated among a beautiful forest, and sits below Kinnerly Peak. Fishing is allowed in Kintla Lake, but closed at Upper Kintla Lake.

4. Packer's Roost to Flattop Mountain and Fifty Mountain

Distance: About 6 miles to Flattop Mountain, another 6 miles to Fifty Mountain.
Degree of Difficulty: Challenging
Elevation Gain: 2,000 feet

The Packer's Roost trailhead is located on a short dirt road that veers left (north) just before The Loop section of the Going-to-the-Sun Road. Drive a short distance on a one-way road to the trailhead. National Park Service rangers use this trailhead to pack in supplies with horses and mules for the Granite Park Chalet.

After about 1 mile on the trail, there is a fork. Go right to ride to the chalet, veer left to ride to the Flattop Mountain area. In my opinion, this trail is of low scenic value for day rides as the first several miles are through forest and the elevation gain is significant. However, if you are willing to ride longer, the scenery becomes phenomenal as the Livingston Mountain Range comes into view and the country is much more open.

TRAIL RATINGS FOR GLACIER NATIONAL PARK

1. Easy-going

- Iceberg Lake
- Bowman Lake
- Kintla Lake
- Upper Two Medicine Lake

2. Intermediate

- Belly River (including Belly River Ranger Station, Elizabeth Lake, Cosley Lake)
- Lee Ridge Trail
- Red Eagle Lake
- Gunsight Lake
- Ptarmigan Lake
- Cracker Lake
- Medicine Grizzly Lake
- Morningstar Lake
- Cobalt Lake
- Old Man Lake
- Fielding Coal Creek

3. Challenging

- Firebrand Pass
- Gunsight Lake to Pass
- Ptarmigan Lake to Tunnel
- Piegan Pass and Siyeh Pass
- Swiftcurrent Pass

- Many Glacier to Poia Lake
- Triple Divide Pass
- Cobalt Lake to Two Medicine Pass

Belly River Area, Glacier

Bison in Hayden Valley, Mary Mountain Trail, Yellowstone

TRAILS IN YELLOWSTONE NATIONAL PARK

Yellowstone is the world's first national park, created in 1872. It is the second largest national park in the lower forty-eight states, with plenty of trails to ride. Today, the park is mostly used by visitors to view wildlife and geologic wonders. However, horseback riding remains a traditional and time-honored approach to view the park. I have found that even on busy summer days, once I mount up and ride down the trail, it is not long before most visitors are left behind and the scenic majesty of the park awaits. Yellowstone is frequented by visitors who like to drive the roads and take photos of wildlife and scenic vistas. More than once, I have had a car stop and a visitor get out and ask if they could take a photo of my horse and me.

Please remember, the numerous tourists that visit Yellowstone are often not familiar with horses or horse etiquette, so gentle explanations are often helpful. Once, I went for a nice ride in Yellowstone and returned to the trailhead. As I unsaddled my horse, a man stopped his car and got out. He asked me if he could ride my horse the next day. I explained it was my personal horse and I was not part of a commercial horse-riding operation. So he offered to buy my horse and ride it. I politely declined.

On another occasion, I planned to ride the Specimen Ridge Trail from one end to the other, about 20 miles. My wife kindly agreed to shuttle the horse trailer from the west trailhead to the east trailhead located near the Lamar River where there is a designated parking area for horse trailers. My wife and I got an early start; I saddled up and was on my way. My wife then drove to the Lamar River parking area to wait for me. She planned to read a good book and enjoy a relaxing day until I returned.

When she arrived, the designated parking area for horse trailers was filled with cars. There was no place for her to park the horse trailer. Knowing there was nowhere else to park, my wife got out of the truck and practically shouted to the tourists walking around, “Hey, can’t any of you read? This sign says this parking area is for horse trailers only, now move!” Apparently the tourists scattered like elk running from a pack of wolves, for in a few moments everyone fled and she had the entire horse-designated parking lot to herself.

If the rider is unfamiliar with Yellowstone, I suggest you visit the park’s web page and review its rules and regulations. There is a section on horseback riding in the park. Also, stop at one of the visitor centers or call the Backcountry Ranger office and ask about trail conditions. For this book, I will start in the northern portion of the park and work around the park in a clockwise fashion.

The northern areas of the park can be accessed through Gardiner or Cooke City. The Eagle Creek Forest Service Campground, located about two miles outside of Gardiner, has several large horse corrals available on a first-come basis. The Elk Fork Campground in the Shoshone National Forest, located between Cody, Wyoming and the East Entrance to Yellowstone Park, also has horse corrals. And there are other USDA Forest Service campgrounds near Yellowstone that have horse facilities. These can be located by searching online or contacting a USDA Forest Service office where the personnel are always very helpful. Facilities and capabilities change over time. Sometimes the Back Country Horsemen, a national volunteer group with state chapters, will identify a campground or trailhead and expend resources to upgrade or restore them that makes horse use much more favorable. Many towns often have fair- or rodeo grounds that allow for overnight stabling of horses when the facilities are not otherwise in use.

For Yellowstone National Park, the following trails are closed to stock:

- Thermal Areas
- Artist Point
- Avalanche Peak Trail
- Beaver Ponds Trail
- Canyon Rim Trails, including Harlequin Lake Trail
- Osprey Falls Trail
- Monument Geyser Basin
- Seven Mile Hole Trail
- Sheepeater Trail
- Shoshone Geyser Basin
- Storm Point Trails
- Tower Falls Trail
- Trout Lake Trail
- Upper Terraces
- West Thumb Overlook
- Wraith Falls Trail

MAMMOTH HOT SPRINGS—NORRIS AREA

1. Cache Lake – Glen Creek Trailhead

Distance: 5 miles
Degree of Difficulty: Easy to mildly intermediate
Elevation Gain: 500 feet

Discussion: Drive about 5 miles south of Mammoth Hot Springs and park on the west side of the road, which is reserved for horse trailers. Parking on the east side of the road is reserved for hikers.

The trail heads west to a Cache Lake, a modest lake surrounded by meadows with Electric Peak looming behind the lake. Electric Peak stands at 10,992 feet and is the sixth highest peak in Yellowstone. This trail has little elevation gain and is very pleasant to ride with easy-going trails. However, be careful to stay on the correct trail to the lake. This is good bear country.

2. Bighorn Pass

Distance: 8 miles
Degree of Difficulty: Challenging
Elevation Gain: 1,800 feet

Discussion: Drive about 8.5 miles south of Mammoth Hot Springs and turn into the Indian Creek Campground. Immediately after crossing the bridge, there is parking for horse trailers on the left side of the road.

After saddling up, you must essentially ride through the campground before the trail turns west toward Bighorn Pass. It is about 8 miles to the pass. The trail is a mix of forest and open meadows, but closer to the pass, the trail is mostly in the forest. The last section of trail to the pass is steep but doable for a capable horse, or simply dismount and walk the final portion. Once atop the pass, the views in both directions are superb and stunning. There are remnants of trees that died in the great fires of 1988—now they seem like ghosts from the past. You can turn around and return to the trailhead, or ride to the west end of the trail on U.S. Highway 191, a distance of about 19 miles, requiring a shuttle.

MAMMOTH HOT SPRINGS—TOWER AREA

1. Blacktail Creek

Distance: 4 – 6 miles
Degree of Difficulty: Easy
Elevation Gain: Minimal

Discussion: At Mammoth Hot Springs, turn onto the road to Roosevelt and Tower. Drive 6.5 miles to the Blacktail Creek trailhead. There is a small parking lot on the northside for cars, but use the large southside parking lot, which also has an outhouse. Alternatively, drive west from Cooke City.

From here, you can ride to the south along a two-track road for about 1 mile to a set of old corrals and buildings. From there, the road disappears but you can follow an unmarked trail to the west and up to the top of a ridgeline, then ride to the south and eventually loop back to the corrals and back to the trailhead. This is a nice ride through beautiful country. Once, as I was riding up along the ridgeline, a lone wolf loped by. I have seen numerous elk in this area, and it is particularly beautiful in the fall when the aspen leaves turn.

Alternatively, a rider can cross the highway from the parking lot and ride north along the Crevice Lake trail. It is several miles to the Yellowstone River. Just before the bridge across the river, go right a hundred yards or so and there is a small log cabin with a hitching post and an outhouse. This is a great location to rest or have lunch, and in and of itself, makes for a nice ride. But if you want to continue on, cross the bridge. You can ride left to Crevice Lake, but it is not very scenic. I prefer to veer right and continue along the Yellowstone River trail. This is a nice place to ride and there are nice locations along the river where you can stop and enjoy the views.

2. Hellroaring Creek

Distance: 4 – 20 miles
Degree of Difficulty: Intermediate to challenging
Elevation Gain: The ride to Hellroaring Creek descends about 1,000 feet from the trailhead to Hellroaring Creek; to the crest of the Buffalo Plateau is about 2,500 feet.

Discussion: The turnoff for Hellroaring Creek is about 14 miles east of Mammoth Hot Springs. There is a short dirt road that is on the left (north) side of the paved road. Take this dirt road down to the parking area where there is room for horse trailers and a hitching post.

From this trailhead, a number of options exist. First, ride down about the trail about 1 mile to the Yellowstone River and cross the suspension bridge. Continue on about one-half mile and the trail will fork. You can ride straight and reach Hellroaring Creek. From there, you can go left or right and follow the trails. If you veer right (east), you will reach a National Park Service cabin in 1 or 2 miles on the far side of the creek that makes a great place for lunch.

Alternatively, you can take go right (north) at the fork and head upward. In another 0.5 mile or so, the trail will fork again. The Buffalo Plateau Trail turns right, while Coyote Creek Trail continues straight. Buffalo Plateau is a broad open plateau that requires elevation gain. The views and wildflowers will make this trip worth the effort. Once atop the plateau, the trail veers to the left. A small creek provides water for the thirsty horse, and the trail becomes much more pleasant. It can be very nice to continue riding for another couple of miles to enjoy beautiful country and solitude.

The Coyote Creek Trail continues north to the northern park boundary, then into the Absaroka-Beartooth Wilderness. Large pack trains can be seen heading into the wilderness. There are some campsites along the way that make great spots for a lunch break.

The two trails can be combined as a loop. From Hellroaring trailhead, ride up the Buffalo Plateau trail to the patrol cabin (about eight miles) and take a rest. Then continue onward to the park border. A sign will mark the location. Turn left or west and ride the Poacher's Trail (National Forest, #98) about four miles until reaching the junction with the Coyote Creek trail, then turn left (south) and ride back to the Hellroaring trailhead (about six miles). The entire loop is about 20 miles. Again, this requires an early start and a well-conditioned horse, but makes for a spectacular and solitary ride. In my opinion, it is best to ride this loop from the Buffalo Plateau trail to the Coyote Creek trail. And please beware the Poacher's Trail is not well-maintained and will require some route-finding. A GPS map would be helpful.

TOWER JUNCTION—NORTHEAST ENTRANCE AREA

1. Specimen Ridge

Distance: 20 miles end to end.

Degree of Difficulty: Challenging

Elevation Gain: A mostly gradual ascent of almost 3,000 feet if riding to the end, or to the top of Amethyst Peak.

Discussion: The trailhead for Specimen Ridge is located about 2.5 miles east of Tower Junction on the road to Cooke City. A large pullout is located on the north (left) side of the road. If that is full, a smaller but useable pullout is located a short distance farther down the road. The trailhead is on the south side of the road.

Specimen Ridge is a beautiful and scenic high plateau that stretches for miles. It can be approached from the west or east. However, it is preferable to start from the west trailhead. The first mile or so involves a sudden and fairly steep climb onto the plateau of Specimen Ridge. For some, it might be best to dismount and walk the horse up the short but steep switchbacks. Once atop the ridge, the riding is more gentle but ever upward. This trail is perfectly acceptable for a well-conditioned horse. In my opinion, this trail has some of the best views of anywhere in Yellowstone and very few people venture onto the plateau. Wildlife are abundant. I have seen pronghorn antelope, elk, bison, bears and wolves on the plateau. Keep a sharp eye out for petrified trees and fragments, but do not take anything with you, it is illegal.

Once, I was riding atop the Specimen Ridge area. A herd of some 75 bison was grazing in an area below a set of trees. A large bull was settled on the ground nearby. Then I watched the bull stand up and slowly walk through the herd. As it did, all of the bison parted and moved out of the way, acknowledging the dominance of the bull. It was as if Moses parted the Red Sea.

Another time I was riding atop Specimen Ridge and encountered a small herd of pronghorn antelope. They ran away from us at breakneck speed for a couple of hundred yards or so, then stopped. My horse and I stood still and watched. Then a most interesting event unfolded. The pronghorn antelope turned to face us, and slowly began walking toward us. As they walked, they continually watched us and seemed ready to bolt at a moment's notice. But they kept coming until they were about 40 or 50 yards away, and formed a semi-circle around us as they all just watched and looked. This went on for several minutes, before they decided to slowly meander away. They seemed most curious. At about the 3-mile mark, the trail divides. A rider can veer right and follow the Agate Creek Trail. Continue straight for the Specimen Ridge Trail. You can also ride to the summit of Amethyst Mountain, or all the way across and down to the east trailhead at the Lamar River. The ride from trailhead to trailhead is about 20 miles. It's important to get an early start and ride a horse in good physical condition. I have done this when my sweet wife shuttled our horse trailer from the west-end trailhead to the east side at the Lamar River trailhead. I then rode from one end to the other. Again, if you are considering this, it is best to ride from west to east.

2. Agate Creek

Distance: 6 miles
Degree of Difficulty: Challenging
Elevation Gain: About 1,000 feet of elevation gain to the place where the trail descends 1,200 feet to the Yellowstone River. Total elevation gain to and from is perhaps 2,200 feet.

Discussion: This is the same trailhead as Specimen Ridge.

At about the 3-mile mark, the trail divides. Take the right fork and continue. The trail passes through scenic and open country for several miles. Bison will almost certainly be seen. But I have also seen pronghorn antelope, elk, grizzly bears and wolves on this trail. At about 5 miles, the trail will descend steeply to the valley floor and the Yellowstone River. The switchbacks make it passable for the horse. There is a park campground about 0.25 mile before the end of the trail. This campground is very scenic and a great spot to rest and enjoy the views. The trail ends at the Yellowstone River. There are a lot of downed trees and it can be difficult to meander around. The fishing is great if you packed a fly rod.

Slough Creek Trail, Yellowstone

3. Slough Creek

Distance: 4 – 8 miles
Degree of Difficulty: Easy
Elevation Gain: 400 feet, mostly within the first two miles.

Discussion: The trailhead for Slough Creek is located about 6 miles east of Tower Junction. There is a gravel road that turns to the north and leads to the trailhead and campground. There is plenty of room for horse trailer parking.

The trail is actually a wagon road used by the private Silvertip Ranch located just to the north of the park boundary. This trail is very easy to follow and has spectacular scenery. In the summer, wildflowers abound. This is a great trail to start with if the horse and rider are new to Yellowstone or inexperienced. Parking is easy and the trail is awesome.

The first 2 miles of this trail are uphill with limited views. Then the trail levels out as it enters the long valley that contains Slough Creek. This is one of the most scenic valleys in all of Yellowstone. People who are fishing are often seen during the first few miles of the trail. However, as you continue farther up the valley, the likelihood of seeing other people greatly diminishes. If you ride far enough, you can ride across the park boundary and continue into the National Forest wilderness area. There are several park campsites located along the trail that make great places to stop for lunch or to relax and enjoy the day before returning to the trailhead.

4. Pebble Creek

Distance: 12 miles end-to-end.
Degree of Difficulty: Intermediate
Elevation Gain: About 1,000 feet, mostly within the first mile or so.

Discussion: The Pebble Creek trailhead can be accessed from a west or east location. The west trailhead is located at the Pebble Creek campground area, about 19 miles east of Tower Junction. There is adequate parking for horse trailers. The east trailhead is known as Warm Creek, and it located on the north side of the road about 1.5 miles east of the Northeast entrance station. On the south side of the road is a picnic area.

This is one of my favorite rides in the park, because it is rare that I see another soul. There will be several crossings of Pebble Creek, but the fords are shallow with good footings for the horse. About halfway through this ride, there is a trail junction to Bliss Pass. This will carry a rider over to the Slough Creek valley, but this trail is not always cleared and maintained. If you plan to ride this portion of the trail, please contact the Yellowstone Backcountry Ranger Office to confirm trail status. A great option is to start at the Warm Creek trailhead, then ride to the Pebble Creek Campground trailhead. This requires someone to shuttle the horse trailer, but it allows for a nice 12-mile end-to-end ride through spectacular country. If riding from the east-side trailhead (Warm Creek), the first mile or so is quite steep, so be prepared to ride uphill or better yet, dismount and walk the horse when steep. Eventually the trail levels out and then descends into the open valley of Pebble Creek and there will be no more elevation gain for the duration of the ride. There are several backcountry campsites that make great places to stop for a break or have lunch, and then you can continue onward or turn around.

5. Lamar River

Distance: Up to 5 miles
Degree of Difficulty: Easy
Elevation Gain: Minimal

Discussion: The Lamar River trailhead is located about half-way between Tower Junction and the Northeast Entrance. There are two large parking areas, one is reserved for horse trailers and the other is for cars. So make sure to park in the correct lot.

It will be necessary to immediately cross Soda Butte Creek. After riding a little over 1 mile, you can veer right and follow the trail to Amethyst Mountain and Specimen Ridge, or continue straight. About 1.5 miles later, the trail will split again. The Lamar River Trail continues straight, while the Cache Creek trail turns left. There are numerous campsites along the Lamar River Trail that make excellent locations to stop and enjoy the scenery or have lunch. This trail is popular with horse riders.

CENTRAL—FISHING BRIDGE AREA

1. Mary Mountain, Hayden Valley

Distance: Up to 6 miles
Degree of Difficulty: Easy
Elevation Gain: Minimal

Discussion: The Mary Mountain trailhead is located about 4.5 miles south of Canyon Village. The pullout at the trailhead is not very adequate for horse trailers, but drive just a short distance farther south and there are additional pullouts on the west side of the road that are much better for horse trailers. From there, you can saddle the horse and access the trailhead.

This trail takes a rider across the northern edge of the spectacular Hayden Valley. It is best to ride this in the fall, as the trail is typically wet and boggy during the summer months. You can ride about 7 miles through open country and fully expect to see bison and possibly a grizzly bear or wolf. The trail then enters forest and continues on to the east trailhead located at the Nez Perce trailhead, located about 6.5 miles south of the Madison Junction. You can ride from either side toward the other side and turn back, or arrange to shuttle the horse trailer and ride end-to-end. This is a nice late-season ride when the higher elevations might have snow.

2. Howard Eaton Trail

Distance: 2 – 4 miles
Degree of Difficulty: Easy

Elevation Gain: Minimal

Discussion: The Howard Eaton Trail is located just east of the turnoff for Fishing Bridge. There are parking areas on the north side of the road.

The trail essentially parallels the east side of the Yellowstone River. This is a leisurely ride and is great for riders seeking a mellow ride without a lot of elevation gain. There are scenic places along the river trail to enjoy the pleasant view.

3. Pelican Valley

Distance: 7 miles to patrol cabin
Degree of Difficulty: Easy
Elevation Gain: Minimal

Discussion: Drive about 3 miles east of Fishing Bridge, then turn left (north) a paved parking lot. There are designated spots for horse trailers, a hitching post, and outhouse. This is a very easy-going trail for the horse. Take this road a short distance to the trailhead and park. During mid-summer, the parking lot can get full, so plan for an early start. In the fall, there will be no difficulty with parking.

This is a very easy-going trail for the horse. In the summer, the grass will be green and the valley will be filled with wildflowers.

The trail begins with about a 0.5-mile ride through a meadow, then goes through the forest for 1 mile or so before entering the broad and long Pelican Valley. From the trailhead, it is about 7miles to a National Park Service cabin with hitching post. This makes for a great ride to enjoy spectacular scenery, have lunch, and then make the return ride. You can also continue another 1.5 miles to Mist Creek Pass. Or you can continue around the valley and ride a loop. However, the trail on the far side of the Pelican Valley is not always well-marked and there are bison trails everywhere, making route-finding very challenging. It is easiest to simply ride the return trip the same way.

Pelican Valley is one of my favorite places in Yellowstone to ride a horse. The scenery is spectacular, and the riding is easy-going.

This trail is closed to all humans until early July, and is open only from 9:00 am to 7:00 pm, to reduce the risk of grizzly bear encounters. This is perhaps the best prime grizzly habitat in the park. Numerous bison are often present as well. You should ride with your eyes alert.

One beautiful autumn afternoon, I was riding through the Pelican Valley toward the ranger cabin at the head of the valley. I spotted a large grizzly bear on the far side of Pelican Creek. I stopped my horse and watched the bear. It was about 200 yards away. All of a sudden, the bear must have smelled us and it stood up on its hind feet to get a better look. The bear seemed large, even at such a distance. Then the bear did something rare and a bit unsettling. It started to move toward us, first at a walk and then a lope. As it approached Pelican Creek, it stopped and stood on its hind feet again to look us over. Then the bear started to cross the creek toward us. Although my horse remained calm during this episode, I felt it was time to move on, so we moved away at a trot and the bear stopped and turned back.

4. Turbid Lake

Distance: 6.5 miles (one-way)
Degree of Difficulty: Easy to intermediate
Elevation Gain: 1,100 feet

Discussion: This trail can be accessed from two different locations. The first is from the Pelican Valley trail, the other trailhead is known as the Nine Mile Trailhead, located on the East Entrance road. The trail to the lake is easy-going and little elevation gain, but not well traveled or maintained. From the Pelican Valley trail, travel about three miles from the trailhead. There will be a trail that turns to the right (south), leading to Turbid Lake. Buffalo are frequently in the area. In mid-summer, wildflowers abound. The lake itself is not very scenic and is acidic and mostly devoid of life. The surrounding area has mudpots that smell of sulphur. Turbid Lake can also be accessed from the Nine Mile Trailhead. From this trailhead, it is about three miles to the lake.

5. Thorofare—East Shore of Yellowstone Lake.

Distance: Up to 70 miles
Degree of Difficulty: Easy
Elevation Gain: Minimal

Discussion: The Thorofare trail contains some of the most remote areas in all of the Lower 48. This trail travels through the southeast portion of Yellowstone Park and into Bridger National Forest of Wyoming. From the Nine Mile Trailhead, one can ride several miles along the east shore of Yellowstone Lake. Views of the lake are intermittent. One can ride several miles or more, enjoy the day, have lunch, then turn around. The trail is excellent for horses.

SOUTH

1. Shoshone Lake and Shoshone Geyser Basin

Distance: 8.8 miles
Degree of Difficulty: Easy
Elevation Gain: Minimal

Discussion: I have never ridden a horse on this trail, but when I inquired with a backcountry ranger, I was informed it would be a nice ride. Once you reach the geyser basin, you need to dismount and explore on foot, as horses are not allowed in the actual Shoshone Geyser Basin area.

MADISON AREA

1. Nez Perce Trail

Distance: 7 miles
Degree of Difficulty: Easy
Elevation Gain: Minimal

Discussion: The Nez Perce Trail is located about 6 miles south of the Madison junction on the road to Old Faithful. The trailhead is on the east side of the road. This trail leads to Mary Lake and can be ridden across to the Mary Mountain trailhead, located in the Hayden Valley.

This is a very easy-going trail with virtually no elevation gain. The trail meanders through open meadows and forest. There are creek crossings, but they do not pose any difficulty for the horse rider. About 5 miles or so down the trail, a large meadow is located on the right (south). This is a great place to stop for lunch and turn around if you do not wish to ride farther. Bison are commonly seen.

SOUTHWEST

2. Bechler Meadows

Distance: 7 miles
Degree of Difficulty: Easy
Elevation Gain: Minimal

Discussion: The Bechler Meadows trailhead is located near the Bechler Ranger Station. It is best accessed from Ashton, Idaho. If traveling from afar, a rider can usually keep their horses in the fairgrounds of Rexburg or Ashton, Idaho. If there is a ranger at the Bechler Range Station, I suggest that you stop and chat before heading out on the trail. Or call the Backcountry Ranger Station and talk with a ranger before making the long drive to the trailhead. There is a good 10 miles or so of dirt road, so if there has been a significant amount of rain, the road conditions might be challenging.

This area is best visited in the fall, as the terrain can be wet and boggy or marshy in spring and summer when insects are numerous and annoying. In the fall, the colors are beautiful. The Bechler Meadows area is also a spectacular place to ride in the late fall when higher elevation locations may be inaccessible with snow or cold weather. The terrain is easy-going and typically passes in and out of the forest.

Park campsites make excellent places to stop and rest, enjoy lunch, or just meditate and feel the beautiful ambience of Yellowstone.

At about the 5-mile mark is once such campsite, 9A1. Boundary Creek provides water and is easily forded. You can turn around at this point, or continue onward. Dunanda and Silver Scarf Falls are about an 8-mile ride.

WEST YELLOWSTONE—NORTHWEST AREA

1. Gneiss Creek Trail

Distance: 8 miles, end-to-end
Degree of Difficulty: Easy
Elevation Gain: Minimal

Discussion: The Gneiss Creek trailhead is located a little over 9 miles north of West Yellowstone. Parking is located on the right side (east) of road. There is room for horse trailers.

The trail is easy-going and travels through a mixture of forest and open country. The views are very nice and there are a couple of campsites that make great places to stop and enjoy lunch before turning back.

2. Bighorn Pass

Distance: 8 miles
Degree of Difficulty: Challenging
Elevation Gain: 1,800 feet

Discussion: The Bighorn Pass trailhead is on U.S. Highway 191 north of West Yellowstone. (You can also access the trail from the east side at the Indian Creek campground south of Mammoth Hot Springs.) If you can arrange a shuttle, it would be a great (but long) day ride to travel from the east side to the west side.

If you wish to simply ride to the pass, I suggest riding from the Indian Creek campground trailhead on the east side, an eight-mile ride, as the ride to the pass from the west side is about eleven miles.

It is about 18 or 19 miles to ride from one trailhead to the other. Both routes pass through very scenic country and make for a great ride, even if you do not ride all the way to the pass. The views from Big Horn Pass are spectacular. The remains of a forest fire have created ghost-like trees atop the pass.

The west side of Bighorn Pass can also be accessed from the Fawn Pass trailhead. There is a cut-across trail that connects the Fawn Pass and Bighorn Pass trails.

3. Fawn Pass

Distance: 9 miles
Degree of Difficulty: Challenging
Elevation Gain: 2,000 feet

Discussion: The trailhead to Fawn Pass and Fan Creek is located north of West Yellowstone or south of Bozeman. There is a large parking area with hitching posts on the east side of the road near mile marker 22. The parking lot is elevated above the trail.

Ride down a short distance and immediately turn left. Horses are not to go straight up the trail, but should veer left and ride to the Bacon Rind Trail. Then turn right and cross the Gallatin River at a nice ford. Continue along this trail and it will merge with the main Fawn Pass trail about a mile from the trailhead. This adds a bit of distance, but is mandated by the National Park Service to protect the early portion of the Fawn Pass Trail.

The next junction is with the Fan Creek Trail, which goes left. This is a great option for a mild trail ride through beautiful open country.

At about mile 5, there is another junction. The Big Horn Pass cut-off trail veers right. You can take this to access the Big Horn Pass Trail. To continue to Fawn Pass, go left or straight. There is a great place to stop and rest at about 0.5 mile or to enjoy tremendous views from a crest that overlooks a valley. This is also an excellent place to turn around if this is as far as you want to go.

The trail will eventually climb through the forest, including several areas of burned forest. Fawn Pass is about 9 miles from the trailhead. There is a National Park Service sign that marks the pass. To the immediate right is a clump of trees and a great area to rest with the horses and enjoy lunch. A small lake set amidst a beautiful valley is nearby, slightly to the east. To the northeast, Joseph Peak towers over the landscape. This is a long ride, but truly spectacular and very doable for the capable horse.

4. Specimen Creek

Distance: 6 miles
Degree of Difficulty: Intermediate
Elevation Gain: About 2,200 feet to Crescent Lake, the first 3 miles have minimal elevation gain.

Discussion: Driving north from West Yellowstone or south from Bozeman gives you access to the Specimen Creek Trail. There is a turn-off on the east side of the road with a small parking area, including a designated area for horse trailers.

The trail offers a couple of options. One fork leads to Crescent Lake, a one-way ride of about 7 miles. The first several miles are mostly flat with nice views and meadows. Overall, the ride to Crescent Lake is not the most scenic in Yellowstone, but the lake itself is a beautiful destination, a great place to enjoy lunch and a high mountain lake. There are reportedly no fish in the lake.

The spur trail to Shelf Lake is quite steep and I would not recommend it for horses.

The other fork of the Specimen Creek Trail is known as the Sportsman Lake Trail. This is a long trail that is not well-suited for day rides. However, it presents great options for those who wish to pack their horse. You can also make a loop and ride to Crescent Lake, then circle around and return via the Sportsman Lake trail. The total distance is about 22 miles.

5. Daly Creek and Black Butte

Distance: 5 miles

Degree of Difficulty: Intermediate

Elevation Gain: About 1,800 feet to the top of the ridge-line, the first three miles have minimal elevation gain.

Discussion: The Daly (sometimes referenced as "Dailey") Creek trailhead is located at the northwestern-most section of the Yellowstone, a little over 0.5 mile south of the park entrance sign. This can be accessed by driving north from West Yellowstone or south from Bozeman on U.S. Highway 191. The parking area is located on the east side of the road. A hitching post is available.

I really like this area of Yellowstone because it offers more solitude than other areas of the park, and there are several nice options for horseback riding, all located in a beautiful area. Most of the riding is in open country with interspersed forested areas. The mountain views are tremendous. Bison are not usually found in this area, but I have frequently seen grizzly bears, along with moose and elk.

From the Daly Creek trailhead, it is a 5-mile ride to Daly Pass. The first 3 miles or so course through beautiful open meadows, interspersed with a few small stands of trees. At about 1.8 miles, there is a trail junction. The Daly Creek Trail continues straight or east, while a cut-off trail veers right to join with the Black Butte Trail.

To access the Black Butte Trail, veer right and continue on for another couple of miles to a National Park Service cabin, located in the forest. This is a nice place to stop for lunch. A hitching post is present. You can turn around and return to the trailhead, or continue a few miles to the Black Butte trailhead located along U.S. Highway 191. The Black Butte trailhead has a small parking area south of the Daly Creek parking lot. Just north of the parking lot for Black Butte trailhead is a large pull-out on the west side of the road that is better parking for horse trailers. From there, you can saddle up, cross the highway and access the Black Butte Trail.

Continuing along the Daly Creek Trail, about another mile or so past the Black Butte cut-off, there is another trail going to the left (north). This will connect with the Tepee Creek trailhead. Continue straight for Daly Creek. At about the 3-mile mark, the trail begins to climb toward the pass and travels through more trees. However, there are small open areas or parks that are beautiful. The trail is very manageable for the horse.

At Daly Pass, there is a four-way junction. To the right (east) is the Sky Rim Trail. It is not recommended to traverse this trail in its entirety on horseback. However, I strongly suggest the rider proceed up the Sky Rim portion of the trail about 0.5 mile or so. It will require some elevation gain, but once atop the ridgeline, the views of the Gallatin Range to the north and west, and Yellowstone to the south and east, are truly spectacular and should not be missed. It is a great place to dismount and enjoy the views and have lunch before the return ride.

You can ride the trail to the left (west) along One Day Ridge. This follows the park boundary down to Tepee Creek in Custer-Gallatin National Forest. Then take the cut-across trail and return to the Daly Creek Trail and back to the parking lot at Daly Creek.

6. TEPEE CREEK, CUSTER-GALLATIN NATIONAL FOREST

DISTANCE: 4-6 miles or longer
DEGREE OF DIFFICULTY: Intermediate
ELEVATION GAIN: About 1,800 feet to the top of the ridgeline

DISCUSSION: The Tepee Creek trailhead is located just north of the northwest corner of Yellowstone. The trailhead has adequate parking for horse trailers and is located on the east side of the highway.

From this trailhead, you can ride directly to the Sky Rim Trail, then down the Daly Pass Trail and forming a loop, return to the Tepee Creek trailhead via the cut-off trail, located on the Daly Creek trailhead. This can be traveled in either direction. This is a very nice trail to just go for a pleasant ride and enjoy beautiful scenery in solitude.

TRAIL RATINGS FOR YELLOWSTONE NATIONAL PARK

1. Easy-going

- Slough Creek
- Mary Mountain/Hayden Valley
- Howard Eaton
- Pelican Valley
- Gneiss Creek
- Fan Creek
- Bechler Meadows
- Shoshone Lake
- Nez Perce
- Cache Lake
- Blacktail Creek
- Turbid Lake
- Thorofare

2. Intermediate

- Daly Creek
- Tepee Creek
- Specimen Creek
- Lamar River
- Blacktail
- Pebble Creek

3. Challenging

- Fawn Pass
- Specimen Ridge, including Agate Creek
- Big Horn Pass (from either side)
- Hellroaring

Slough River Trail, Yellowstone

CONCLUSION

I feel very blessed to have had the great opportunity to ride good horses in country as beautiful as Glacier and Yellowstone National Parks. It is a dream come true. In the countless times I have crossed paths with hikers along the trails, or interacted with park visitors at trailheads, virtually all have expressed their admiration of my horse and some envy of the adventures that my horse and I have in the parks.

I WISH EACH OF YOU THE SAME FEELINGS OF JOY.

Happy Trails!

ICEBERG LAKE TRAIL, GLACIER